JUST LET ME WORSHIP!

How worship can transform your life!

JUST LET ME WORSHIP!

How worship can transform your life!

ALICIA MOORE

Atlanta GA

Just Let Me Worship

©2021 Alicia Moore

All rights reserved. No part of this publication may be reproduced or transmitted in any form or by any means without the written permission of the publisher.

ISBN:978-1-7358124-6-5

All services completed by Imprint Productions Inc.

Printed in the United States of America

Published by Imprint Production INC.
info@imprintproductionsinc.com

Christian Life
First Edition 2021

10 9 8 7 6 5 4 3 2 1

CONTENTS

ACKNOWLEDGMENTS 1

INTRODUCTION 5

1 FOCUS ON JESUS! 11

2 FAR OFF WITH A PLAIN VIEW INSIGHT 23

3 A DIVINE APPOINTMENT 31

4 A TRUE WORSHIPPER 39

5 EVIL SPIRITS RECOGNIZE AUTHORITY 45

ABOUT THE AUTHOR 51

ACKNOWLEDGMENTS

First, I want to acknowledge my Heavenly Father, Yahweh, for equipping and empowering me to birth out this project. I am elated and humbled that he has allowed me to also emerge as an author. He does all things well. Never give up on yourself, for surely it will come to pass. He that hath begun a good work in you will complete it.

I want to acknowledge all of those who pushed me, who would not allow me to give up, and held me accountable for completing this project. You know who you are. You constantly prayed for me and my ministry and went to war on my behalf. You encouraged me to remain focused, and most importantly, you believed in me, and that meant everything to me.

I want to acknowledge my birth parents, the late Harold Dean and Alice Faye Burroughs, for birthing me into this world. You didn't know that you birthed an Author, did you? Well, you did! You both are gone out of this world but never from my heart.

I want to acknowledge my late husband, Pastor Eddie H. Moore, Junior. You were here with me when I first started the manuscript. I remember how you would always push me and let me know that I could do this. You never gave up on me. You saw the best and more in me than I could see of myself at that time. I'll never forget your labor of love for me.

I want to acknowledge and give double honor to every Prophet an Apostle who prophesied and declared the word of the Lord over my life. You saw into my future, released the word of the Lord, and now it's coming to fruition. This is only a portion of the many declarations that have come to pass. The best is yet to come.

I want to acknowledge my wonderful Church family, Hope and Manifested Glory Ministry, and all of my family, friends, and co-laborers in the gospel for just simply being a part of my life and taking this journey with me.

Thank you, and I love each of you. Shalom.

INTRODUCTION

Have you ever found yourself in a position where all you had was your worship to rely on to bring you through some of the most challenging moments in your life? I have. There were moments when I felt too weak and burdened down to pray. There were times when I didn't feel like preaching, teaching, or even really hearing anyone else. But, I just knew that if I was going to survive, I needed to get into the presence of the Lord. The wonderful thing about getting into His presence is that you can find peace from your torment, strength when you're weak, and so much more.

Your worship is what ushers you into his presence. Worship is the vehicle that leads to intimacy, and when there is intimacy, something powerful is conceived and birthed. For example, when you first enter, you may be experiencing mental torment. But by the time you come out, you will have received peace that surpasses all understanding. Sometimes all I had was my worship that ushered me into the presence of Yahweh. I've been misunderstood, rejected, abandoned, abused, afraid, alone, battered, betrayed, broken, confused, endured mental anguish, endured attacks of sabotage and character assassination, publicly humiliated, and walked through valley experiences, just to name some. There were various situations from my childhood up into my adult life where different life issues caused me to experience these emotions.

While going through these situations, sometimes I didn't have anyone to talk to who would understand, so I just learned to talk to the Lord.

I noticed that every time I fell on my face in worship before Yahweh, something would break off of me. During those times in my life when a sermon couldn't help, a prophetic word didn't matter, prayer wasn't what I was interested in doing, and besides, I was too heavily laden to even pray for myself. There was a moan and a groan of agony and pain that could not be uttered nor understood by the natural mind. There was nothing nor anyone who could help during those moments to take it away. There were times and seasons where I felt stuck. I was gripped by fear, paralyzed by the sting of pain, and I couldn't move out of that place. Sometimes I didn't want to move, and sometimes I was too scared to move due to the fear of the unknown. Money, things, or stuff couldn't help, nor did they.

I used my God-given ability to be able to be alone and be okay with being alone as an excuse to stay away from others, but it was misappropriated and misused. My gift, which was meant to help me maneuver in my mandated calling, was not supposed to be used to cover up my issues.

However, to me at the time, that was my mechanism to get me through what I was enduring. But eventually, I learned the difference and how to balance in that area. Sometimes we can hide behind our gifts and talents until we run into a brick wall and reality hits like a ton of bricks. At that point, you realize that you have to face the truth about yourself, live a life of hypocrisy, or deal with your issues in order to be set free and live a life of liberty.

I felt like the woman with the issue of blood. Wait a minute! I was that woman with the issue of blood. Though my issue wasn't a physical outward bleeding disorder, I'd been cut and injured, and I was oozing with blood on the inside. Smiling on the outside but so sick and disconnected from society on the inside. I ran from people just to isolate myself because I didn't know who I could trust anymore; the wounds were so deep, and I was used to being rejected and misunderstood and just didn't want to subject myself to further pain. It wasn't easy facing the giants standing before me because I had to relive some of those painful moments and deal with them. I couldn't preach over it, praise it, or teach others over it any longer. I had to face the truth that I was a mess and that I'd run out of options. I even had to endure more of the process while writing this book. There are some situations that people can't help get you out of; only the Father can do that! These were experiences I had to walk out of and processes to endure to get to know Abba (The Father (God)) in a greater measure.

I was in some low places of humiliation. One thing about being on the bottom, you can't go any lower, and you can only go up from there. So, I had to go deep to the core of the sore, to scrape the bottom of the wound that had developed from the pressure. The only thing left was for me to fall flat on my face prostrate before Abba in worship and just pour everything out to Him. Nothing else mattered; I just needed to worship because I'd begin to learn that that was my place of deliverance.

During my worship, the Father never failed to soothe my aching heart and give me the breakthrough that I so needed. Sometimes you can't be strong for others, not because you don't desire to but because you don't have the strength. Being that woman with issues, I had a tiny glimmer of hope. I knew that if I could just press through the mess facing me and get into the presence of my High Priest, who could not be touched by the feelings of my infirmities, I knew that I would be alright. I knew that I would find safety and receive the necessary deliverance and strength to go on in life. It's okay to take a step back until you get healed and regain strength for yourself. Just like the demon-possessed man knew that if he could just get to Jesus, a change would come. I personally knew, if I could just get into His presence, I would be alright. Have you felt like I felt? If you did, it's okay. I just kept hearing myself say, "Just Let Me Worship."

In this project, we will discover how worship keeps you in Yahweh's presence which ultimately brings about a transformation in your life. I want to explore another life-changing encounter with you! It's about how worship can change your life! So, sit back, relax, get your box of tissue and let's take a little journey together as we embark upon *Just Let Me Worship.*

CHAPTER 1

FOCUS ON JESUS!

Mark 5:6 But when he saw Jesus afar off, he ran and worshipped him.

It's interesting how people who are possessed with demons or those who don't look like, smell like or act like those who are already inside the Church building get kicked to the curb. Jesus said they that be whole need not a physician, but they that are sick. Often, those who are in dire need of deliverance are the very ones who get overlooked most of the time. However, those who are sick are the ones who will benefit the most from the anointing that is upon your life. It is imperative that we, the body of Christ, begin to see each individual through the eyes of the Lord with unconditional love and look beyond the issues and see their needs. In addition, when people encounter you, they should sense something different about you. If the spirit of the Lord is truly on the inside of you, it will be noticeable. In doing that, respect for the vessel being used comes automatically; however, that is not our focal point. Though we are willing vessels that the Lord may use, we want to always be sure to exalt the Lord Jesus and bring glory to him. However, you may very well be the one holding their deliverance.

There are so many reasons that we have for which we worship Yahweh.

However, in this unique encounter, I want to focus on a demon-possessed man who worshiped Christ and received a complete life overhaul. This is a perfect example of how one's life can be totally transformed and renewed through worship. Notice that he was not exempt from worshipping the Lord because he was demon-possessed. This is an indication that even people who know that they have issues can worship the Father. In addition, many times when we read this story, we tend to only focus on the fact that the demons in the man recognized Jesus' authority, and so true, he did. But there is so much more insight into this story than just the recognition of authority. Even more importantly, it's what took place in this man's life once he submitted himself to the authority he recognized. One can recognize authority, but you cannot benefit from the one in authority until you submit to the authority. One day as I began to reread this event, the Lord gave me a more profound revelation regarding this demon-possessed man. He enlightened me regarding how an individual can receive total deliverance in their life simply through worship, and I want to share it with you.

Although not in his right mind, the man knew enough to know that there was something different about Jesus. He knew that Jesus was not just an ordinary man but that he had in his possession what he needed, power to be delivered. We know that Jesus operated in power and authority, and the man recognized it also. When he approached Jesus, Christ didn't dismiss the man, but he confronted and dealt with the unclean spirit in the man. We must be cautious not to harm but to care for the person and deal with the spirit.

Further in this encounter, we come to know that this man was totally out of control and that no one in the city could control him. He dwelt among tombs, he broke fetters and plucked away chains, night and day he was in the mountains crying and cutting himself with stones. According to society, he was a crazy mad man. But when he laid his eyes on Jesus and got in his presence, something powerful happened; not long after that encounter, he became a controlled man. He entered into a position and atmosphere in which he could receive deliverance. Anytime you're in the presence of the Lord, deliverance can come. How was it that his obscene behavior came to a complete halt once he got in the presence of the Lord when all of the other times, no one could keep him and his behavior under control? He came into the presence of power and authority. This is indicative that we should seek to get in the presence of Jesus and get his attention and not just mere men.

Anyone who encounters Jesus is bound to experience change. *The scripture says, But when he saw Jesus afar off, he ran and worshipped him.* He moved in a hurry. He didn't procrastinate, but he ran. He didn't move at a slow pace; he ran! When you recognize that you are in need of help, you should move quickly. In spite of all of the people in the town who knew his current state and most likely did not know what to expect him to do next, he saw, recognized, and ran to Jesus, the only one he knew could help him. Specific individuals are often drawn to you by the spirit of the Lord because you may be the one designated to help them; you may be holding their deliverance. We should not become fearful when a demon-possessed person approaches us. Let's not be so quick to dismiss people with issues who desire to get close to us. First, find out the reason why they desire to get close to you. It's most likely because they see Christ in you. You may be their only help.

Test Yourself Question!
(Please be honest with yourself because this is between you and the Lord)

1. Have you ever allowed people's opinions to stop you from coming to Jesus, getting in his presence, and worshipping him the way you desire, despite your condition? If so, why?

_____
_____
_____
_____
_____
_____
_____

If so, why?

_____
_____
_____
_____
_____
_____

If you have made that mistake in times past, please do not allow yourself to make that mistake again. It's okay... be encouraged. Let's move on, shall we?

One must acknowledge that they have a problem before deliverance can take place. As we can see, it is imperative that we first get to Jesus. Not only did he move quickly, but once he got to him, he worshipped. What does worship look like? Worship is not only a clapping of the hands, stomping the feet, or just singing a song. Let's get a clear understanding of what worship means in this particular scripture.

In this scripture, the Greek word for worship is "Proskuneo (pros-koo-neh'-o)", which means to kiss like a dog licking his master's hand. It means to fall upon the knees and touch the ground with the forehead as an expression of profound reverence. It also means to prostrate oneself, to do homage to one, or to make obeisance to express respect or to make supplication. I want to take it a step further and give the definition for worship in the Hebrew language. "**Shachah**" (pronunciation:

shaw-khaw), the Hebrew term means to bow down, to depress, to prostrate oneself before a superior in homage, to give obeisance, and to do reverence to royalty or God.

Ultimately, worship is a position of the heart, and your physical position is an outward expression of what's taking place in your heart. There must be humility of the heart in order to worship. The Father is summoning his people to worship him like never before; He seeketh for such. We see that the unclean spirit in the man recognized that Jesus was one to whom reverence should be given. The fact that the unclean spirit requested of Jesus not to torment him was an indication that he recognized that there was a supreme being with authority standing before him. He paid homage and respect to Jesus; he worshipped the savior. Demonic spirits recognize and respect authority.

This man came straight to Jesus in spite of his condition. He didn't need anyone to coerce him to go to Jesus, nor did he allow anyone or anything to hinder him from getting there, though no one would have gotten in his way at all. Let me encourage someone right here, in spite of your current condition, find your way to Jesus and get in worship mode. Remember, worship means to do homage to one or to make obeisance, either to express respect or to make supplication. Please do all you can to get in his presence.

Approach the Lord reverently. Don't come before him with an arrogant, haughty spirit but come humbly, submit and revere him. God resisteth the proud, but giveth grace unto the humble.

You will find that when you do this, things about your present condition will eventually begin to change. For this man, his whole life changed within moments. The scripture declares that after the unclean spirit was cast out of the man, those who fed the swine went out to see what was done. They were afraid because they saw this same demon-possessed man sitting and clothed in his right mind. Can you imagine how much of a mess he was when he approached Jesus? Yet instill he worshipped him, and the Lord honored it. What am I saying right now; your worship is not predicated on your condition!! Your worship does not need to sound or look like anyone else's; it just needs to be sincere. For so long, many people have felt that they weren't worthy to worship the Lord because they may have been dealing with specific issues in their life or just felt lost. Or perhaps they may not have reached a certain plateau in their spiritual walk with the Lord, thus feeling inadequate. No matter what condition an individual finds themselves in, all are welcome to reverently approach the Lord in worship.

One does not need to be perfect in order to worship the Lord because none of us are perfect anyway, though, at some point, one should try to do better and show their heartfelt gratitude towards the Lord. However, those are the very ones that need to worship him because worship leads you into the presence of the Lord, and magnificent things can take place there. In fact, these are the people whom he desires to worship him.

A certain woman by the name of Mary Magdalene was healed of evil spirits, infirmities and seven devils were cast out of her.

She ended up financially aiding Jesus in Galilee. She showed her appreciation and gratitude. Sometimes, desperation leads to sincere worship. Your spirit may not be clean in the interim, but when it's a genuine cry, Jesus takes notice. You might not have it all together at that time, but when you're earnestly seeking the Lord, it leads one to worship the Lord truthfully because you understand that truthfully you just need to capture the Lord's attention. The spirit in you may be unclean, but your mindset of humility is what the Lord sees. So yes, worship him with the right spirit and in truth. Your truth may be that you have issues. Your truth may be that you don't have it all together. Your truth may be that you are sin-sick. The Lord wants honesty and nothing fake; he sees your heart. If you are a mess, tell it to the Lord. He knows already anyway; he just wants us to acknowledge it and depend on him for help.

Man looketh on the outward appearance but the Lord looketh on the heart. Just like the man we are discussing, he had an unclean spirit, but he sincerely desired something from the Lord and absolutely got his attention. Unfortunately, some have the heart to want to do better but feel unworthy to come to him. But the truth is that Jesus desires to bring deliverance into the lives of his people, but he wants to be acknowledged as Lord and Savior. You can't receive something from someone whom you don't believe nor receive. Again, Jesus came for those who are sick and in need of a physician, not for those who are healed and whole. We have all been in this place before, in need of healing one way or another. There are many instances in the Bible where sick people paid homage to the Lord, and he had compassion on them and healed them. There is just something about worship that breaks the mold. Make it your business today to just worship the Lord. Tune everyone and everything else out and capture the Lord's attention. Come to him as you are, worship him, and deliverance will come. I declare that you won't remain the same, in his holy name.

CHAPTER 2

FAR OFF WITH A PLAIN VIEW INSIGHT

To think of an object being far off is to believe that the object is unreachable or unattainable. The scripture says that this man looked out and saw Jesus afar off. Jesus was still some distance from the man. In order for him to see Jesus afar off, he had to fix and focus his view on the individual coming towards him. It is a must that one gains the ability to see beyond what they may see in the mirror currently and see who

Yahweh is getting ready to make them to be. That was a prophetic word right there! It's called faith. Faith is believing that you can become someone whom you're currently not.

Let me say it like this regarding the man in this discussion; basically, he looked beyond his current situation and affixed his eyes on Jesus, the only one who could transform his life. Jesus is the solution to every issue. We can use this man's experience as a great example for many today! Look beyond your current circumstances and see the need for Jesus. It takes a level of faith when a person can look beyond their issues and recognize that He is ultimately the one who can deliver them from their issues. I'm sure that this man had heard about Jesus before now. He'd heard about the miracles and knew what Jesus was capable of doing, and knew that Jesus could help him. Everyone had heard about Jesus! I wouldn't doubt that this man hadn't also seen Jesus in action. No matter how much of a lunatic he was, it wasn't enough to keep him away from getting to the Lord. He forgot about his issues, looked beyond them, and looked to Jesus. It is a tactic of the enemy to keep us focused on our problems and not to focus on the problem solver. It was something about him that caught his attention. Just like us, when we first heard the word, it was something different that we'd never heard before, but it captured our attention and caused our eyes to become opened. This man had an encounter with the living word.

Day in and day out, this man was being tormented by unclean spirits. Apparently, he wanted help because he ran to Jesus and not from him. There was a sense of urgency and expectation as if he was waiting for the deliverer to come. He looked out, and there was Jesus in his view. When a person gets desperate and realizes that they need deliverance and can't find an answer in any other source, they will search for the help they need. It will cause one to look beyond their present condition and seek help. Don't be ashamed to pursue help from the Lord and his anointed ones. Jesus died so that you can be set free from the demonic powers of darkness. People may look down on you and think that you don't deserve to be free or changed, but the Lord sees differently, and he will not cast you away. Freedom belongs to you, and the Lord wants to set you free so that you can serve him and be a witness to others of his saving grace. Not only does freedom belong to you, but he also has a plan for your life. He sees you, knows your condition, and understands where you're located in your life right now, and he will meet you right there. Come to Jesus just as you are. Don't wait or delay any longer. All he wants you to do is seek for him and cry out to him for help. The Lord is nigh unto them that are of a broken heart; and saves such as be of a contrite spirit (Psalms 34:18).

Test Yourself Question!
(Please be honest with yourself because this is between you and the Savior)

2. How did you handle coming to Jesus even though you felt so far off from him and felt that you didn't deserve his grace?

_____
_____
_____
_____

Test Yourself Question!
(Please be honest with yourself because this is between you and the Savior)

3. Do you currently feel distant and far away from the Lord?

_____
_____
_____
_____

Do you need to draw closer to him now?

_____
_____
_____
_____
_____

If so, what steps do you think you need to take to do so?

_____
_____
_____
_____
_____

    I want to encourage you to do all you can to draw closer to the Lord. He's waiting. You're going to be just fine. It's okay...be encouraged. Let's move on, shall we?

    You may have felt so far off from him, and your life may be in shambles, but he's able to fix you and your life. Many make the mistake of trying to fix and perfect themselves first but remember, that's the holy spirit's job. He just needs you to come to him. Jesus came to set us free from our sin, not to save us once we become free. We can never become perfect on our own, so we need to invite the perfect one to abide on the inside of us. We need the power of God operating in our lives. Coming to Jesus is an indication that you recognize that you are in need of being saved or delivered. If one is perfect and has it all together, do they really need a Savior? But we are all as an unclean thing, and all our righteousness are as filthy rags (Isaiah 64:6)

CHAPTER 3

A DIVINE APPOINTMENT

In the natural sense, an appointment is an arrangement to meet someone at a particular time and place for the purpose of exchanging information for improvement. Appointments are also made for meetings, correspondences, and conferences. They are utilized to give and receive information to accomplish a goal. A divine appointment is a meeting with another person that has been specifically and unmistakably ordered by God. This was a divine appointment made by the Lord on behalf of this man.

The Lord's timing is perfect in each of our lives. The demon-possessed man did not have the ability to make any appointments, but he knew when it was his appointed time. The Lord knew that there was a day of deliverance coming for him and that on that day, he would be totally set free from the enemy's control. He would no longer be the same uncontrollable person that society knew after having his encounter with Jesus. There is an appointed time in which we shall encounter the saving power of Jesus Christ. Everyone's timing may not be the same, but know that Yahweh has set your timing. There is a set time appointed for every individual in this world who seeks the Lord's help. The appointment is set; you just have to get there. Yahweh has a plan for all of our lives that is attainable if we allow his will to be done. The length of time for which one has been in a particular condition doesn't matter and has no bearing on your set time of deliverance.

The scripture reads in Mark 5: 5

And always, night and day, he was in the mountains, and in the tombs, crying, and cutting himself with stones.

This man had been in a deep dark place in his life for a long time. He was also chained down and ran around like a mad man. He was out of his mind and was daily being tormented by unclean spirits. But one day, he looked up and saw Jesus. He recognized who he was and already knew that Jesus was not just an ordinary man. He was someone who could help him!

When spiritual scales drop off of your eyes and you become enlightened, you begin to see the necessary things you need, things that will benefit you, your life, and those around you. When you meet your appointment with Jesus, it will be a life-changing event. It will be like no other experience that you've ever encountered. Everything about you changes, and you become a new creature. Therefore, if any man be in Christ, he is a new creature: old things are passed away; behold, all things are become new. II Corinthians 5:17.

When you encounter your divine appointment with Jesus, strongholds are loosed, yokes are destroyed, and you become a changed individual in totality. Please understand that it's the enemy's job to keep you from this very place because he does not want you to be set free from his power. The enemy uses a tool called shame to try and get you to isolate yourself. To stop you from getting into the presence of the Lord. He will make you feel guilty to the point where you feel that you don't even deserve to be in the Lord's presence. He will do all that he can to block and prevent you from receiving your deliverance. This is why we find that many people over the years have run from the church building. They have been made to feel *you must be perfect* before coming to worship. Isn't it wonderful to know you don't have to wait until you enter a building to have an encounter with Jesus? You can encounter him wherever you may be and not only just in a Church building. The spirit of Yahweh is omnipresent. He's everywhere and can locate you at any time. In addition, we must understand that worship is a mechanism and a precursor for deliverance. I'm not against church buildings at all, but if for some reason you are not able to get to one, it does not mean you can't have a meeting with the Master.

However, no one can blame anyone for keeping them away from the church because when you are desperate enough, you'll get there in spite of what anyone says or thinks. Sometimes you need to seek out the anointed vessels of Yahweh to get the help that you need. The trick of the enemy is to make you feel so unworthy to the point where you don't feel you have the right to ask the Lord for anything, let alone be in his presence. He already knows your heart and knows what you need. Your worship is an indication to him that you realize you need the Savior's power operating in your life. So, press beyond the wiles of the enemy and get to your destined divine appointment.

We understand that this man was tormented by evil spirits day and night; evil spirits torment people. They are not your friend! It was never God's intention for demons to enter human beings. When the fallen angels were kicked out of heaven and the fall of man occurred, this catastrophe took place. From that moment on, they have always sought for a body to invade and reside. The enemy is the prince of the power of the air, but his agents need someplace to live. Once a demon has entered a body, its ultimate goal is to torment the individual and keep them in bondage. It doesn't necessarily want to kill the individual physically. To do so would demolish its domicile, and they no longer have that particular body to live in anymore. However, they can lead one to physical death because of their conduct. A spirit cannot live in anything dead. It needs something that is breathing, living, and thriving to abide. An evil spirit will live in a person until they are cast out. They can live in a body for a very long time. Sometimes people are not aware that an evil spirit is abiding in them. They've become so familiar and comfortable with it until they don't even know there can be a difference. It takes an anointed individual with a spiritual eye to see beyond the person, detect the evil spirit, and confront it.

When demon-possessed people have an encounter with the Lord, it is at that time that the evil spirit can be cast out. These spirits are subjected to authority. We know that Jesus will never again return to this earth, so he has anointed vessels in the earth's realm with Christ-like attributes who walk in the same authority and has the ability to cast out evil, unclean spirits and help you get to your deliverance. Today, God uses his ambassadors to help bring forth deliverance and set people free, when the time is right. The person must submit to authority, as we witnessed the way this man did in the text. Someone who operates in kingdom authority and power must take authority over the unclean spirit and cast it out.

Test Yourself Question!
(Please be honest with yourself because this is between you and the Savior)

4. Have you encountered your divine appointment yet?

_____

If so, what took place during that time?

_____
_____
_____
_____
_____
_____
_____
_____
_____
_____

If you are reading this book and have not yet encountered your divine appointment, I'm declaring that not many days hence you shall have a life-changing meeting with your Savior.

CHAPTER 4

A TRUE WORSHIPPER

The word of God declares that they that worship him must worship him in spirit and in truth. However, before an individual receives deliverance, they are more than likely worshipping out of desperation, but worship is worship, no matter how you slice it. According to the scripture, even the demon-possessed man worshipped the Lord. We were all born with an inclination to worship; it's just that many choose not to. In addition, we are not the ones to determine whether it's artificial or genuine. God knows the heart of every man. Therefore, we must allow the person to worship to the best of their ability and the way they know how to, despite their present condition, because worship can bring a person from a dark place to a place of enlightenment and, eventually, intimacy with the Lord.

Truth can proceed from someone who's living in darkness. However, this is the part that one must come to a conclusion, realize and understand; they need to be altered because their truth is coming from an impure place mixed with foreign matter, an adulterated place.

Until deliverance came, it was the voice of the evil spirit speaking through the man. An evil spirit can speak the truth even though it is not from the spirit of truth. It knows the truth, but the source behind the voice is not from the spirit of truth. Remember the damsel in Acts 16:16, who was possessed with a spirit of divination who followed Paul and Silas many days saying, "These men are the servants of the Most High God, which shew unto us the way of salvation." The words spoken out of her mouth were true, but it was an unclean spirit speaking through her. Remember, fallen angels, also known as unclean spirits, dwelt among the truth before being dismissed from heaven, so they know the word. This is why they can twist or give parts of the truth and deceive people. They know the difference between right and wrong, a falsehood, and the truth.

An individual becomes a true worshipper with a pure spirit after deliverance, giving their life to the Lord, and the spirit of truth has come. Once the individual becomes the Lord's possession, evil spirits can no longer possess and torment them permanently. First, however, it is vitally important for the individual to repent, confess that they belong to Jesus Christ, and maintain their relationship with the Lord to keep every void filled.

The devil hates worship unto God because he understands how powerful worship is and what worship can do. Do we recall that he was once the head worshipper? He now wants to be worshipped. He no longer has the privilege to worship God, so he constantly tries to stop and block the people of God from worshipping Him. He wants to take away from us what he no longer has the right nor privilege to do. Unclean spirits know and understand that they have nothing to do with worship and that they will not be able to remain in the presence of the Lord once a person enters into worship. Worship to any evil spirit is just like a pesticide to an insect.

It causes them to flee because they can't tolerate the presence of holiness. Worship torments evil spirits. Once we set an atmosphere of worship, portals for signs, wonders, miracles, and demonstrations begin to open and flow. The atmosphere becomes a prime one for evil spirits to be evicted. There are times when you can't wait for anyone else to set an atmosphere of worship for you, but you have to enter in for yourself. This man set his own atmosphere. Jesus didn't wait until the man was delivered before he was allowed to worship him. The man was demon-possessed as he worshipped Jesus, but his worship brought forth his deliverance. Just as the Lord moved for this man, he is waiting to move on your behalf also. Once you have received your deliverance, don't let your worship stop but be sure to continue to worship and praise the Lord.

Mark 5:7 says, *And cried with a loud voice, and said, What have I to do with thee, Jesus, thou Son of the Most High God?* The spirit knew that he and Jesus had nothing in common and that he couldn't remain in the presence of Jesus without being confronted. The spirits knew that Jesus had authority over them and the man. They recognized that they were trespassing and in a vessel that was ordained and made to worship the Lord. The unclean spirits understood that their season of abiding in the man was coming to an end, and the only other option they had was to submit and leave. This brings us to another point that evil spirits know when their time is up. They sense when it's time to evacuate and exit the premises. Either they will submit or run. The scripture said he cried with a loud voice. Who cried with a loud voice? The displaced spirits cried out with a loud voice in fear that they were getting ready to be dismissed.

It was the man who worshipped Jesus, not the spirits because they didn't want anything to do with Jesus. Only a worshipper wants everything to do with the Lord. The man wanted to be free, but the evil spirit didn't want to let him go. The man had sense enough to know that he needed to be free and realized that only Jesus could make him. When this man had an encounter with Jesus, his life completely and immediately changed. No one comes into the presence of the Lord and leaves the same way they came. When you encounter Jesus, your life will change.

Take this man for an example. Consider his response to Jesus's presence.

First, when he saw Jesus, he ran to him. Secondly, he approached Jesus in the condition that he was in but in a position of reverence. Thirdly, he worshipped the Lord.

CHAPTER 5

EVIL SPIRITS RECOGNIZE AUTHORITY

Mark 5:7 I adjure thee by God, that thou torment me not.

Evil spirits know those who have the right, power, and authority to cast them out.

The evil spirit spoke out and said to Jesus, "Torment me not." The Greek word for torment is basanizo (pronunciation: bas-an-id'zo) which means to question by applying torture, to vex with grievous pains, and to harass and to cause pain. This spirit did not want Jesus to do to him the exact thing he was doing to the man. Evil spirits are not your friend. They hate you and only want to destroy you. They only come to kill, steal, and destroy. The evil spirit knew that he was trespassing, and the way he was tormenting the man was illegal, unwanted, and vile. The spirit was aware of his actions and the way that he was causing the man to act. Demonic spirits are not stupid, but they are knowledgeable and very much aware of what they are doing. For that spirit to make known that it did not want to be tormented is an indication that it was aware of its own actions.

Please be mindful that there's also a right time and a wrong time to approach evil spirits. Even the Legion in the man knew; that's why he stated, "have you come to torment us before our time?" When spirits are confronted and dealt with, they are being tormented because they don't like to be confronted.

They want to be left alone to have their way, act how they want to act and remain in the place they have taken their abode. Please don't allow them to remain in you. Freedom belongs to you! Be set free and made whole today.

Disclaimer:
Please note that this book does not encourage anyone to remain in sin and just worship the Lord anyhow. Accept Jesus Christ as your savior. Give your life to Him. Begin living for him and serving him. Seek for deliverance. Seek for a change to take place in your life as you enter into the presence of the Lord and begin to worship him. I pray that as you have read this book that a change has already taken place in your life. It is also my prayer that you have gained a deeper understanding of your eligibility to worship Him. Worship the Lord, and begin living your best life of holiness with him.

Test Yourself Question!
(Please be honest with yourself because this is between you and the Savior)

5. Please share with yourself what, if anything, you've learned or gained from this book!

_____
_____
_____
_____
_____
_____
_____
_____
_____
_____
_____
_____
_____
_____
_____
_____

A few nuggets regarding worship

- Your worship unto the Lord can usher you into an atmosphere that is conducive for deliverance so that it can be brought forth in your life.
- You may have an issue, but when you have a true encounter with Jesus, you won't leave his presence the same way you came.
- When you encounter a person in need of deliverance, first get them to acknowledge that Jesus is Lord. Wherefore I give you to understand, that no man speaking by the Spirit of God calleth Jesus accursed: and that no man can say that Jesus is the Lord, but by the Holy Ghost. 1 Corinthians 12:3
- Worship requires you to come out of your comfort zone and enter into a place where you're not accustomed to your flesh going, but go there anyhow. Press into his presence.
- Although the Father seeketh true worshippers, he still does not reject those

- with issues from worshipping him because he knows the heart of every man
- The reason you were a worshipper before you received deliverance is because you were created and predestined to worship God.
- A true worshipper worships Yahweh from within, in spirit, and in truth.

If you can't say anything else, or you don't know what to say, always remember that you can say

Just Let Me Worship!

ABOUT THE AUTHOR

Apostle Alicia Moore accepted Jesus Christ as her personal savior at a young age. During her teenage years, she received the promise of the Holy Ghost. The Lord called her into the Ministry and began using her in her early adult years in miracles, signs, wonders, and preaching the gospel. Over the years, she has operated in the office of an Evangelist and, some years later, was affirmed as a Prophet. She is going on ten years as the Founder and Pastor of the Hope and Manifested Glory Ministry Church located in St. Petersburg, Florida. In the year of 2020, she was affirmed as an Apostle, and she is now a prolific revelatory Teacher as well. She operates in a spirit of excellence and believes in giving God her best. She is now an Author and a focused and purpose-driven anointed Woman of God who has proven to be worthy of the calling and mandate on her life. Through manifold trials and temptations, she still stands. She has made her calling and election sure! She is a Global Apostolic Ambassador for the Kingdom of God, and she is well on her way and in pursuit of fulfilling that mandate. The world awaits her! Surely the hand of the Lord is upon her life.